Company of Women:

New and Selected Poems

Company of Women:
New and Selected Poems

Jayne Marek
Lylanne Musselman —
Mary Sexson

To Mono,
Enjoy your Company of Women!
Best Wishes,
Mary Marek
5/13/13
Terra State Community College

Chatter House Press
Indianapolis, IN

Company of Women:
New and Selected Poems

For information:

Chatter House Press
7915 S Emerson Ave, Ste B303
Indianapolis, IN 46237

chatterhousepress.com

ISBN: 978-1-937793-15-9
Library of Congress Control Number: 2013936088

Also by Chatter House Press

beyond first words
Penny Dunning

Street Girls Have Guns
Gregg DeBoor

Battle Scarred
Jason Ammerman

Almost Music From Between Places
Stephen R. Roberts

Some Poems To Be Read Out Loud
Richard Pflum

Many Brave Hearts
Virginia Slachman

Muntu Kuntu Energy
Mwatabu Okantah

Inside Virgil's Garage
Lindsey Martin-Bowen

World of Mortal Light
Virginia Slachman

Jayne wishes to thank the residency program at Playa, where some of these poems were written. She dedicates her work to Joe, with love.

Lylanne wishes to thank her Company of Women cohorts, Jayne and Mary, for their friendship, support, and for sharing the page and stage. She also wishes to dedicate her work in this book to Ann, who has been and always will be an inspiration, and to Glenn, the best friend ever.

Mary dedicates her work to Jack, for his unwavering love and support.

CONTENTS

PART I

THE UMBRELLA SHORE

Jayne Marek

Trapping Season

One evening in October
when I was just nine,
the old fields breaking
along the mud lane stippled
with the paths of muskrats,
Grandpa let me watch
how it was done. The day
was raw, fit for the dark fur
of clouds with their eyes of rain.

He had eight or a dozen of them,
trapped by the crick, and one by one
he chopped off the head, the paws
like needles bundled in black velvet,
then sank the blade into the secret, the smell,
making crossings through the pale
belly, and a slit at the tail,
then he hung on tight and peeled.

As he worked the big blade
flashed like Captain Hook. The skins
were like mittens bleeding inside out,
corpses the size of dolls, the joints
like newborn birds' wings
mottled by cold air
they're not ready for. Learn early,
Grandpa said, and spat. Blue and pink
the inner bags glistened, the
spattered dirt walls gleamed.

I watched death cut and opened,
felt the bite of the drawn-out
ritual seaming, that turning
the garment to get another wearing,
while floorboards above us groaned
under the feet of the women
in the kitchen, and the lantern light
wavered over the skinning and the stairs.

Quality Control

Once in a factory
with machines in one room and
metal pieces and box forms in the next

where I sat with the
other women checking
hundreds of toothed white wheels an inch

across, listening
to the Lebanese woman calling us all
crazy — *shedonna* — the feminine ending — a noise

from the packing
area tables, like the box
stapler thump only gentler,

was the head and then
a scuffling sound, the feet of an older
woman down against

the two-by-four table legs
that hemmed her in
in the blue afternoon time under

long hanging lights too
poor to show either what you're working
on, or true shadow —

believe me, if you know
someone cheap, you know the light there —
she struggled for

twenty seconds in what
had to be filth, and then the men
from the punches pushed

up the machines' levers one
after another and hurried
over to cradle

her head and bumper
her arms during the rest
of the fit, but

the manager
                     who always watched us women
no matter the work, wouldn't
let us get up. As if

his saying, "It's taken care of"
made that true, as if any words can
take or make

more than the eye with its
parallax
of encroachment

and calculation. You don't
know who will at last
see you in the slant

darkness of your own making.
Shedente, the Lebanese woman
whispered, flicked her wrist.

Fitting

Imagine it unwinding from a slowly rolling bobbin, a thread
to baste the long ears of wheat before harvest day,
the making before the need of winter clothing.

Imagine the fit of this gold grass, like one's best suit,
intimate as secret folds under arms,
the measure of the living and dead known to certain hands.

Imagine the track of cutting shears like a fresh haircut,
lapels lying flat along a ditch edge in the wake of reapers,
warp and woof of the field pressed together, and still warm.

Range in the Stars

For a minute I drift into the photograph of distant mountains
at dawn, a lavender peak afloat above another ridge, dark purple, the whole sky
dusted with pink, the nearer landscape in maroon, its tree and cactus shapes
emerging. The January cold of Arizona surprised me
during my first visit, held me in a clinch. I learned to love that cold
as my mother loved this mountain range, the Sierra Estrellas. She could sense
how every day the mountains breathed far away, rising from either side
toward the single crest above the dry Valley of the Sun. Even hidden
by smog, some days, the mountains were there, her privilege,
a place she would go to some day, she said. In the photograph, the range gently
draws a line between lingering gloom and the rising light.

Encounters

I

I encounter them every day –

Dad when I enter the hardware store,
Benevolent and mild as a pail of blue paint,
Familiar as scents of sawdust and cut metal,

Mom entering the doorway of a shop
Strung with earrings like trinkets
That she will be pleased to give me –

In the edge of a familiar chin
In a passing car, or the shape and color
Of someone standing quietly in an old jacket.

II

Sidewalks the night after his funeral
Were empty as if steps had passed and led to
One of the small neighborhood houses.

Her carnival-glass vases and candy dishes
Rested atop lace doilies on a dining table
For the cousins to choose from and take home.

Everything is as it was in unimportant ways.
Finding without finding again,
The movements of loss.

If I Really Think About Your Death

— after Patrizia Cavalli

So, then, against your pause
that expected a one-more love
I hung up.

I slid around the word,
a bare sprig
in torn-up ground.

Yet didn't we both know it needed
saying? To take each other's hands
again—yours like wedges of bruised fruit,
your arms a struggle of veins,
your neck slack,
ashamed
to have been found old—
this time, ending so much time,
knowing that, now, never is our condition?

Long ago, rough fencing marked
the edges of old yard
that had been lush as four forests
growing hard on all sides,

the house at the foot of a hill,
blankets of violets,
elms of the mind's eye
under which you leaned, raking yellow green
fractured leaves,
calling me to come down.

I did not come down
to help you.

Beyond grass and backyard flowers,
lilacs stumbled against the garage,
flagstones toed the plum trees.
At sunset, the split window in the lean-to shed
kindled — one break
too many.

If I really think about your death

through the chilly air of the past
I would float toward you now,

everything will flow on earth like fall's leaves
in their hundreds, broken
but returning
for another year,
filling the yard to its borders, covering
the edges,

so we can gather before the wind can steal.

In March

Orion sinks behind the ridge
the owl's voice opens
she is dusted blue in the moonlight
in early spring
there is a sound her heart desires
like the wind
in dry weeds revealing a presence
that is ancient
how many times has this owl
told the tops of pines
counted the stars between pine needles
the hunter yearns
for the sound to trigger her launch and glide
to seize a small thing
to fulfill this night
spark of the senses
that leads into silence
thoughts staring into the deep
familiar always new
a night full of wings of life and death
clouds crossing the moon

Burn Series

I Burn Area

What if I were to climb the slopes of the mountains today
to find the place where light folds under the clouds
that skim the outcroppings this morning of half sun
and keep going letting the dimness surround me
lead me through damp weeds from rock to rock shadows
one at a time they become visible only when I move forward
and finally emerge higher into the daylight
where snow outlines stumps along ridges I have not yet climbed
I would be a transparent wing above the cloud line
among the dead trees marked by fire
touching their shells wondering why some burned black
and others white why some fell in crossed patterns
as if trying to escape to left or right
they all died but it was years ago and the quiet
fog has passed over them hundreds of times
concealing them an act of grace
I would move among the trees recognizing them
one by one alone and mute

II Sunset Clouds

Huddled together the slide area hills   give up their glow
and settle into tender slumber   like chickens gathered on their shelf
quieting with a few   murmurs as when wind traces a contour

through the pass between ridge and mountain   a wing of gold light
unfolds along the flank of a hill   near the top amid the scarred
trunks in the burned area that have not fallen   most bare and limbless

the dead trees   remain at attention watching
signals of the sunset hidden   behind western ridges tipped in pink
and violet nothing else   this evening except for a cloud

of green and yellow grosbeaks   dropping through black branches

III Up There Day and Night

The dead stumps warn each other with their remaining limbs
    they signal for water
ready to carry it   as if they were the multiplying brooms
in "The Sorcerer's Apprentice"   lines of them rallying on the steep
slopes of charred pumice   but no music begins
the ones that still have twigs   reach in seventy directions
with witch fingers   and like very old people sunken
into their own bones   they do not mean to frighten
but the headless stumps   did not survive
they trace on the sky night and day   we did not survive

The Jump

The world
bells underfoot
in sudden silence,
like humanity
itself rarely seen
from distance,
the way
motley fields
stitch their patterns,
beautifully naïve,
is what there is
to love, and the snug pull
is the harness
hugging my body
as close as bones.
The patched world
spreads its furrows
and lifts trees,
like toys,
to the size
of fingers, then hands,
whole limbs,
a descending wind
brushing stray hairs
from my cheek,
my feet dangling
over expanding earth
that reaches for them
with palms of stone,
that turns aside

its tartan field
to a gravel shoulder,
that stops
smiling as feet
step over
the first treetops,
the sudden
ringing of wind
between body and ground
as I close
the space,
the bad landing.

A Lost Country

The six-gun man sitting cross-legged
on the floor of the living room has a face
pleasant and blank as the teevee screen.

It's late. The bowl on the floor is empty. He leans
forward toward the light, now and then whispering
three or four blunt words

to the posse in his mind. He touches the holster once
and softly laughs. Along the riverbank
he has imagined the riders pass, and now

their tracks fill with snow. Silver gathers too
along the old dog's muzzle, along the rim
of the worn ten-gallon, around his spurs

glinting like embers. Sounds settle down
into camp for the night. A lone voice
is muttering the dream of a dark room,

like television late at night, after
the cowboys have all ridden away,
the blizzard moving in.

The Buckskin

Along the high desert road
I came solitary
my breath a harsh signal
of the altitude as I ran
slowly
creating the only sounds not made by wind
and dry grass

passing a paddock I noticed
the horse as it noticed me
its black tail and ears raised
it snorted
and stamped
surprised by the unfamiliar human running

it understood
motion if not reason
feet drumming
we went the same direction
for a time sharing the wind

it outpaced me
turned and came around again to run
at my shoulder
as if to guide me toward
a road ahead
a road not yet perceived

at the fence it stopped letting me go
I wanted its thoughts
to follow me for a mile
around the base of the bluff
and more distant
places where I will be
remembering
looking forward together

Mantis

I

Shuffling on tired feet at the end of the day,

I glanced out the front-door window into early night
And saw yellow legs and a slim peapod body with the unmistakable
Double bump of eyes at one end. The young mantis

Balanced delicately on slipping tiptoes in the light
That shimmered to the edge of the pane of glass
And struggled to climb higher toward the overhead bulb

Tufted with cobwebs, batted by night-flying bugs.
The mantis tried to step with tiny hooked feet.
Again and again, in the same pattern, front legs started

Left, right, and middle legs, alternating, then the back legs,
First one, then the other, grazing across the smooth surface to get
To nowhere new. As it shifted, it turned its goggle head

with glossy pea eyes to watch the movement
of my face behind the door, shifting and reflecting.
Surely its balance was compromised by all it saw —

My eyes and the tip of my nose, glass surfaces, insects flitting —
That might have pitched its vision into confusion.
It seemed ten minutes before it paused.

Then with a soft touch I opened my front door and slid
Out, holding my breath, keeping the door steady,
To stand in a yellow nimbus alive with fingertip

Touches from minuscule bugs' wings at my ears and neck
And along my cheeks. The mantis' head twisted
But it did not flinch when I raised my hand and gently

Propped its left middle leg. The needle tip of its foot accepted
And pushed up, and we waited while the other legs had to lift
In their turn, right middle, the back legs, and finally

The front legs moved and reached the window frame.
It crawled up the rest of the way and hunched, as still
As a green twig after a puff of wind had passed by.

As long as I stood there, it did not grab and eat. Cautious
Or tired or patient, it folded its arms close under its jaws.

II

Meanwhile, I couldn't stay out all night. I went inside,
Probably sat in front of the television, or picked up a magazine,
since lately I haven't felt like reading books.

The stories I want these days are shorter, a full-sized
Page or two, right to the point—simple-minded, even,
Requiring little effort. I get tired early and catch

Myself in a vacant mood, unfocused, eyeing a random item.
I own too much stuff, and now it owns me. The color of lamps
In the living room bores me and pours all over,

And every surface seems nice and soft, a place to sit forever.

Temporary Calligraphy

In a Beijing park, elderly gentlemen in polo shirts, neat slacks,
and baseball caps

Murmur Chinese in low tones skimming beneath the music
that dances

With circles of grandmothers in stretch pants. Along one edge
of the park

In the shade, two gray-headed men wield black brush sticks
like canes

Animated at the tips, dipped in pails of liquid, sketching
calligraphs

On sidewalk squares. Solemnly a third man bends at one writer's
shoulder

As the script ends with a flourish. Both men nod, and the watcher
clasps his hands

Behind his back, while the writer stows stick in bucket
and walks

Unhurried toward a public spigot. The clouds over Temple of Heaven
glow blue

At their bases, show gold along their temporary ridges, line the wooden
struts

Of the circular tower with its knobbed cap, slip between shifting elm leaves

As summer heat slowly dims the damp characters on concrete, lifts them into air.

India Gate

The women in saffron, yellow, indigo and red
Silk saris that rippled as they turned
Like huge flower petals
Or tropical fruits, or parrots' wings

Lovely and whole –
Not like the ragged wings of the scavenging
Kites, dusty brown, spread like broken smiles,
Showing gaps for the tormenting sun –

Those women, carrying plastic trays
Of bead bracelets and necklaces
And wearing twine and bead ankle bands
That ticked against bits of brass,

Stopped and bent to pick up
Some small tokens they had dropped,
Then straightened and looked forward
Without smiling, caught in their moment

Away from tourists, three women together,
Poor but in their best, fabric
Of that burning country,
At the India Gate where the police

In dark uniforms watched everyone
Without seeming to, where great shabby birds
With hook beaks stooped atop
A pillar of neglected meanings.

A Short History of Enchantment

(The boy Lorca encounters a Roman mosaic)

Why my brother why do you not believe
that the spring soil gave
itself spreading its body
to the new steel plow

Papá and Luís let me follow
as it cut the old land
of eyeless sorrow
under a day moon

you were not there!
Francisco, why at your books!
Fool, fool
when the tongue of steel met the lips of the field
they spoke me
gravel coursing the furrows' cheeks

a cry!
The horses' muscles sweated black
the *vega* struggled against the tool
lifted a thick corner
Papá, Luís shouting
as I saw first

los fabulosos, hook-footed lions
blue dropping blossoms, yellow and green vines
black owl eyes
in girls' white faces
like all the stars of summer
weighting a square stone

Francisco my brother
no one could pull me away

a rabbit of shadow
dived beneath the slab
a smell of violets
lichens
saffron and sulphur wings

Francisco it was I
the shadow within my mouth

I fell
and you could not reach me
beyond the branches
of the olives,
light on the other side
of the *sierra*

After Verdun

...the blooming orchards near Verdun
cannot escape
the approaching atmospheric front.
(Wisława Szymborska)

I

In France
we listen to approaching weather
that tore its rags climbing the far cliffs
and mutters, stalking across farmlands,
lashing the henhouses with bean tendrils.

Earth knows what's coming.
Its hollow eyes shut
under the ranks of identical trees
patient in olive cloaks.

Across our automobile windows
oncoming clouds
crowd the road to the restaurant.

II

A stork stalks our lawn table,
shifting its canvas wings.
Each step forces a sign.

Uphill, the vineyards begin to boil.
We bumble against each others' limbs
as waiters snap up glassware
and run. Wind slams the door.

There's a sliding glimpse of the stork
yanking the hat-shapes of napkins
so they hop, flinging pellets of rain.

Laughter hard in our guts.

The bird opens its gray wings,
appeals to the wind
and is gone
in pines.

Thunder pushes red wine
back in our throats.

Múzeum-korut

Coal fumes blue as evening.
Footfalls knock along the cobbles.
Storefronts press shoulder to shoulder

wearing their mottled capes.
We turn a corner near the museum
where we have seen the decorative shrouds

of the dead, the heirlooms of families
whose women's fingers crocheted
those shrouds, now in the alcove cases—

displays of grayed photos
show the stitched cloths around
dead ivory faces, dark hair and brows—

yellow with age, these cloths,
a symphony of holes
breathing heavy odors of wax.

Arm in arm, we enter the alley
with the smell of death on our clothes,
our lips shaping an ancient cant:

*Old world, fetid, slipping a green drip
down the well rope,
let go of my throat.*

From Emptiness

Something called to me
in a voice like an old gourd singing
on its hook by the well
and said
the water is bitter with ice,
it is all you have.

I looked and saw clearly
down the cold bore to the bottom
of earth and litter.

But reach down and lift, something said
and because the clouds were ancient
with what they held
I did,
and it came to my hand,
this time filled.

Invitation

Feel as if you have breasts whether or not you do.
The first points of your body, they push through the weather of eyes
in every room you enter, every day. It's a zöoish connection
like the shape of prey flashing across the eyepan of a dog.
It's also

like having two soft palms spread open to press into the soft belly
of life you stumble toward.
They want what they want and want something else tomorrow.

Your breasts are gibbous moons with half a face veined in them,
two halves.

In release they swing gently like saddlebags, or like
a pair of doves edging a rooftop deciding for flight.
Some days they ring slightly like a china cup lifted from a saucer.
Some days they pull into you with such power they are extra muscles
to help you work.

The pleasure of your strength doubled and raised

The Umbrella Shore

As in the rain the blue van in which we were riding crossed a bridge just as mist shifted to show the long shores of a creek curving across hectic light-green winter meadows, the way grass sometimes is in the British climate, my brother who was driving and I, in the midst of his son's chatter and ditto sounds of a handheld electronic game machine, and his wife as she rattled open the map to see where we had last been before we became lost along this country road because there weren't many signs and we were trying to find our way to the town which was built around mysterious stones, and why would they mark the roads?—they don't want us there, caught a glimpse to the left of a row of opened black umbrellas the size of huts each leaning toward the water's edge, with long wands of fishing poles just visible through rivers of raindrops' paths driven by wind down the windows, umbrellas enormous as exotic blossoms, bells, a long pattern wavering across pale background, and he and I both at the same time said, "We should stop and take a photo of this," and we didn't

and it wasn't just the weather
I've often remembered

PART II

WHAT SHE TAUGHT ME

Lylanne Musselman

Our New English Teacher

— For Ann Johnson

In ordinary Indiana,
unnoticeable on a map,
rural air marked the spot
where a two-story brick building
scraped the sky above the corn stalks,
and fielded our back to school hustle,
fresh from farm communities
in the autumn of 1971 –

As sophomores, seasoned in classroom routine,
we settled in for more Shakespeare,
and lessons on grammar
designed to modify our mistakes
of our misplaced youth
and unpunctuated boredom.

But a new teacher shocked us
out of our parenthesis,
her clothes splashy
exclamation points, a dash of
drama in a room full of drab denim,
whose presence, walking the hall,
made the hardwood floor sing
her entrance, elevated the class
where she cast our adolescent insecurities
or juvenile cockiness aside.

We signed contracts for grades,
vowing to be more than average –
we rivaled each other with renditions
of *Catcher in the Rye* and *Animal Farm*
without the usual prompts or props;
by studying the lyrics of Carole King,
we unraveled the canonized poets,
and with each unfamiliar assignment
we wrote our way out of ordinary.

In My First Fifty Years

I have seen the sky knitting
its cover with strings of light.
I have seen squirrels tumble,
clowns of the lawn.
I have seen the seven of clubs,
flipped face up, trump my thoughts.
I have seen my black kitten's head stuck
in a milk crate so tight
he looked as if he was being convicted
at a witch trial.
I have seen my own heart break
in time to build room
for real love.
I saw reality TV
40 years before its popularity --
Lee Harvey Oswald's
final face, grimaced,
shot dead, live on camera.
I have seen poverty
pick its own sweet pockets.
I have seen police
high speed through low limits
in their leisure suits.
I have seen my love drunk
in a twelve-step dance
with addiction.
I have seen Chatty Cathy
lose her voice
in a game of Tiddly Winks
against Uncle Wiggly.

I have seen September
shed leaves, and chill my lattes cold.
I have seen my stretched skin
marked by the drum
of the womb.
I have seen people shuttered
by an image.
I have seen a dying page
breathe on its own.

Something to Crow About

I

The old woman wants a pet that swoops
and caws its wisdom from high
city rooftops or hidden within
the forbidden maze of cornfields.
She watches a winged flock
mock the tattered scarecrow, limp and static.
Amused, she blows kisses
in the wind, hoping one will land
on her special crow –
she holds out her hand.

II

A young girl cuddles her tabby cat
she calls El Gato. She learned Spanish
in third grade and proudly recites
her feline knowledge to anyone who'll listen.
Cats are drawn to her and she draws cats:
fat cats, small cats, pink cats, polka dot cats,
cats with purple flowers, cats with birds in their mouths,
cats she can't know
resemble Picasso's.

III

Two cats watch out the picture window,
twitching tails in unison, charming birds
they want as their own. The large glass reflects
their inside anxious eyes, and
the outside truths of July –
the sky blinds them blue, the mockingbird
swipes another song and the turtle doves hip hop
across their lawn.

Robin Reflection

--inspired by Jayne Marek's photograph "Robin"

Robin doesn't care
about the Biggest Week
in American Birding
where humans come
from all over the world
to see pretty birds.

He doesn't worry about warblers,
yellows, striped, butter butts,
Baltimore orioles. After all, who is
still around after all those birds
have flown over this flyover state?
Who is the first bird that struts
his stuff because spring is here?

Robin knows he's a dandy –
why watch those common
blackbirds, common starlings,
or dull American sparrows hang
out in your suburban yards?

Robin is rockin' it,
soaking in the reflection
of the most handsome bird
staring back at him
as if he were Narcissus.

The Owl and My Willpower

"Over there, look!
A Great Horned Owl –
can you see it?" asked
the Magee Marsh tour guide.

Over the top of those
cattails in the willow tree,
where the tree forks to the right,
where the limbs form a cradle.

"Honey, your camera's not powerful
enough to see it, use these
high-powered binoculars."

When the crowd thinned,
I scoped out the owl. I saw it
through my little lens and snapped
a couple of photographs.

At home I downloaded my digital pics –
there was the Great Horned Owl,
big as life, looking my way,
with its binocular stare.

On Seagulls

I have to live near seagulls.
I don't know why – being born
and bred in land locked Central Indiana,
but my favorite vacations, and
now where I live near Lake Erie –
gulls rule. They make me happy.
Some people despise these gulls
as dirty, pesky scavengers –
rats with wings. I see them
as freedom, laughter,
warm memories, the promise
of sunny days. These majestic birds
with angel wings in flight, their
constant caws and squeals are a delight
when I see them swooping low
over Toledo - in Metroparks, over city streets,
floating on the Maumee River,
gathered in massive congregations
on the beach before flying away –
flashing the public
their energetic sermons.

Painting the Park

Frogs swim across
the pond, camouflaged
by lily pads and water plants
green as spring trees.

Unsuspecting squirrels
steal raw shelled peanuts,
washing them among waddling
woodchucks and big bully blue jays.

Red cardinals flash
around their flamboyance –
even the softer females
flaunt their crowns,
queens for the day.

A tawny deer mommy
moves two fawns
through shrubs and
branches, quietly
fading into the back woods.

Unexpected Visitor

Lovers came and went,
but for eighteen years you graced my lap,
you slept next to me, and followed me
around the house. You didn't care
if the dishes were done, or if
I gained a few pounds, or shed a few tears.
You were there, a purring anchor –
even as your spirit was leaving me.

Jonathon, you came to me
in a dream last night, strong,
healthy and handsome. You
ascended the wooden stairs
coming up out of the basement,
ran into my open arms.
You reveled in my touch,
I cried your name –
my one constant.

Take Back Time

Give me back my grandma's voice
weaving words, threading my mind,
unfolding tapestry of our heritage.
Give me back the days
spinning a stack of 45s
in Davy's room,
discovering "Pretty Woman,"
singing along with Roy Orbison,
no regrets.
Give me back my hard thighs
flying over the hurdles of my youth.
Give me back my ability to eat a Whopper at noon,
drink regular Coke all day,
indulge in pie on a whim,
never gaining an ounce.
Give me back my passion for painting
before repetition turned to cinders,
canvassing the country
selling art for profit.
Give me back the happiness in the whiskers
of my cat's chin, lying on my forehead
prior to his passing
to perch on a cosmic cloud.
Give me back years wasted
married to men I did not love
for reasons not yet acknowledged.
Take back the years of being stupid,
never being able to do anything right
because my daughters' father said so.
Take back the years of trying to please

anyone who was not me.
Take back the years of lying
under the weight
of my conscience banging the headboard.
Take back the dresses I despised,
frilly and femme, unflattering,
never finding a hem I could tolerate.
Give me back the friendly manner
I possessed until I locked the door
after too many knocks
from those that entered
before I was ready.
Give me back.

Love, Love, Love

I laugh at the idea of love.
I hear Delilah on the radio schmoozing
with callers on her all night love fest
as I drive, from Indianapolis back home
to Toledo, passing the hours by listening to sappy
tales of romance – what a joke,
as I relive past loves with each love song
she spins into the air so sweetly.
I don't love the idea of love anymore –
this once hopeless romantic
truly has had enough of the "Silly Love Songs,"
like the ones that McCartney and Lennon sold
in catchy tunes for impressionable youths
to believe in the perfect love, the happy ever after,
the match made in heaven, the kind of romance that never ends,
"Love Me Do," "From Me to You," "Love, love, love…," and after all
the failed attempts at romance and wedded bliss,
I certainly don't "long for yesterday," or a late night
chat with the love seductress, Delilah.

Our Night Out

In a dark bar on a Toledo Saturday,
too early for the happening crowd,
too late for two friends who decide to stay
in a place that pulls our memories
from "far-out" places – the music patronizes
our middle-age while still flirting with youth –
swigging liquid courage, musing over *Dancing
in the Dark,* and "Who's going to drive you home,
tonight?" Remembering loud nights
that didn't seem too long, way back when,
when we were not paying attention to time,
tick, tick, tocking forward. Our minds reflecting
refracting pieces of our disco selves unraveling
like an off track 8 track tape and when we twirl
around we see each other in the bar mirror –
cynical and dark.

Ode to Aging Baby Boomers

We were wooed by commercials
depicting us as the hip Pepsi Generation,
yet we taught the world to sing
in perfect harmony by simply sharing a Coke.
We were the change the world needed –
no more prejudices. We got Archie Bunker
with his outdated bigotry in living color, and loud Maude,
finally, as women were allowed "to roar."
We were exposed to artificial
Christmas trees, those silver ones –
with color psychedelic wheels; we ate Jiffy Pop
popped in flat aluminum pans that expanded – resembling a Cone head
from outer space, and drank Tang because astronauts did.
Sonny and Cher were sharp contrasts to Frank Sinatra and Doris Day.
Cher's long hair swished the hem of her micro mini-skirt,
Sonny's moustache the type Burt Reynolds stole as ...*The Bandit.*
It was far out when Alice Cooper sang "School's Out for the Summer"
and we were nearly "Eighteen." Everyone knew we were
the groovy bunch – Mike and Carol Brady proud – can you dig it?
Back then *1984* seemed "So Far Away" in our future,
and when The Beatles sang "Will you still need me,
will you still feed me when I'm 64..."
we never imagined we'd get so old.

Consolations After the Death of My Kitten

--after James Tate's "Consolations After an Affair"

Chattering at shadows on the ceiling,
my cats run room to room.
They see little Teddy.
As we settle down at night, he visits.
And I can hear peaceful cats purring,
the love that moves me.
I've discovered that I don't need
a lousy spouse, a loan to repay.
I have unfinished paintings
that wait for van Gogh to return.
They know nothing of sangria and Vonnegut.
For them a foggy night in February
is a ghost of an excuse.

Resurrecting Poets in 2012

If she was alive in 2012,
would Elizabeth Bishop turn,
on television, and confess
to Ellen that her poem
"Breakfast Song" was written to her
much younger female lover?

Would Walt Whitman drive a Smart Car,
sing of wind turbines and America's Obama,
join Greenpeace, and pitch free range farms
across the grassy plains?

Would Amy Lowell ride along with Dykes
on Bikes, appear on the cover of *Cigar
Aficionado*, dine on Jenny Craig
to tone down her size, and spin, spin, spin
at a poetry slam?

Would Emily Dickinson rival Lyn Lifshin
in publishing poems, while hiding
at home writing daily blogs –
or would she find her way out,
read in crowded auditoriums,
enjoy lively book signings, and fly home
to a wife in Massachusetts?

Adios Cursive Writing

Farewell slanted, loopy letters,
pushed across the page
forming well-rounded thought,
our John Hancock signatures.
So long praise for good penmanship,
or penalties for illegible scribbles,
writing with a personal touch.
Salute the writing world's new ruler –
keyboards that process words to march
like soldiers in uniform font and size,
where only **bold** ones stand out
in the crowd.
From now on will writers
of cursive be hailed as artists
and simple handwriting be
the new calligraphy?
Will the art of handwriting
fade into the shadows
of some museum
dedicated to archaic rituals –
along with rug hooking
and candle dipping –
where curious onlookers
study handwritten journals and
love letters scrawled in longhand,
marvel such primitive marks
and scratches but are clueless
how to decipher the words.

Wasting Away in Compositionville

If a genie gave me three wishes,
I'd wish for another hour in the day
to write more poems
feed my wasted muse,

who becomes weaker and more delirious,
hour after hour, I grade packs and stacks
of student papers – papers that defile language,
defy grammar, choke on analysis,

paragraphs that meander nowhere and back, and *there* –
they meant their, they're so sure of themselves:
boastful of how they hate to write, and what does reading
have to do with writing anyway?

I wish they'd just once read something I assign –
Oops, Another wasted wish! Did I just lose my chance
for a long vacation in Spain, or for a carefree year in Paris,
or just some free time to feed my hungry muse?

Lost: Art

Recently at a gallery in Chicago,
David asked:"When did you become interested in art?"

He didn't know, in 1962, my kindergarten teacher
pulled mother aside because of a ladybug I'd drawn,

or that I'd won first place in third grade
for my abstract picture of a cat, á la Picasso,

or that my high school art teacher revered my work,
and assured my doubting mother I had talent.

David didn't know my love of art gave me a high
that drugs never did, and saved me, more than once,

from adolescent suicide, or that art held my hand
through three divorces and dark, pitched nights.

He didn't know I'd become torn between the painting pull
of portraits and the word tug of constant poetry, or

that my perfectionism refused art's playful invitations.
How could he know I shoved my first love away?

Gesso

--to the painting "The Fields I Flew In" by Sarah LaBarge

Beneath the paint
I hold the trees to the canvas,
and I stretch myself out,
providing the ground
for mixed faces to grow old.
I am the glue
for everything but myself.
Most would call me plain.
I'm not visible –
the white space on a poet's page
rich with the lack of words,
or striking –
the way the burnt sienna feathers
beneath the blaze of the rooster's cockscomb.
I size up that whisper of contrast –
flesh and timber,
movement of arms and leaves –
I am the understated bond.

An Aging Game

-for Ann and Jack Johnson

Upstairs,
with my two young daughters,
Jack, entertaining them –
all three singing "Ring around
the rosy…." Their giggles.
His laughter. The shuffling
of feet above. Our tears
of laughter when we heard:
plop, plop, thud,
"we all fall down."

Ann and I
in her art studio,
downstairs,
making handmade paper jewelry.
I remember Jack falling.
Fondly.

Now, at eighty-six, fragile Jack
isn't entertaining. A torn Ann
artfully learns the craft
of caring for a husband,
twelve years her senior:

his crying,
her crying,
that oxygen tank,
those angry accusations,
the constant "babysitting"
the wheelchair pushing,
his unintentional falling down.

What She Taught Me

--for Ann Johnson

I

If she hadn't been that teacher
who pushed me past my limits,
made me give a voice to purple,
in front of the class, who praised
my Polka Horse block print and
asked to keep it for her own,

who gave me unlimited hall passes
signed AJ, to ditch my dreaded Home Ec
at the end of the school day to come
to the art room, where no one cared
if I could sew a stitch, or sauté an onion.

If she hadn't been that teacher
who flunked me for not painting
by deadline, who teased me
out of my shell, who didn't turn me away
when I dropped by her house to say "hi,"
dressing so funky that
she didn't care who stared.

If she hadn't been that teacher
who was vibrant and different,
in school convocations, who dared
to show vulnerability, I would not have
kept going back to school,
each day a new reason to live.

She gave me opportunity to see some world
outside of rural Indiana, first Toronto,
then Niagara Falls, Buffalo, Chicago with art
club – a first airplane ride, a first
subway passage, a first time not feeling lost.

II

If she hadn't been that friend
saddened by my dropping out
of college to marry a man, then
a few years later helping me
get back into art by sharing shows to enter,
new techniques to try and didn't "I told you so"
when I told her I was filing for divorce.

If she hadn't been that friend
who gave me a job cutting and coating
handmade paper jewelry in her studio
so I could support myself and my
two young daughters,

who told me to drive during rush hour
in the heart of Chicago, who sent me to the MOMA alone,
while she manned the art booth in New York City,
who trusted me to drive her, after major surgery, to Twin Rocker
for handmade paper supplies, through blinding snow –
it wouldn't be our last trip through rough weather together
living through damning "Bible skies."

If she hadn't been that friend
who encouraged me to write poetry
when I doubted that I could, who spoke
of *Writing Down the Bones,* and suggested
over and over that I re-enroll in college
twenty years after I gave it up –

If she hadn't been the one –
strong, independent woman
who lead me by example:
accomplished artist, mother, teacher,
businesswoman, world traveler.
When I didn't believe
in me, she did.

PART III

MEMORIES OF AN UNARCHIVED PAST

Mary Sexson

Driving to Town, Sunday Morning

The sparseness of the trees
across the soybean field
allows the sifting of sunlight
through morning fog until it lies
splayed across the still green leaves.

I am driving east, past fields I have known
since childhood, following an old map
inside my head. The memories are dappled
as with sunlight, some shadowy areas
interspersed with crisply defined pictures,
the boy in the casket, the child at the door.

I alternate between holding the pictures back,
denying them full view, and coloring in
the missing details. I am simultaneously
fascinated and repulsed by this
mental video which has neither a rewind
nor a pause button. For there is risk of falling
head first into the memories of an unarchived past.

We mine the heart so carefully day to day
scrutinizing ourselves a hundred times
to keep the feelings in check, the emotion
wiped off our faces. But we neglect our own
attics, and closets, where the sweaty ugly
messy scenes are stored on old chromatic slides,
not held neatly on some glossy iPad with
4 gigs of memory dying to be accessed.

But the map we made as children, the one
with blue lines that shows the side roads
and secret shortcuts is the one I want to follow
today. I want to take the road that goes past
the lake, the one where I can look through
the trees and glimpse those slivers
of shimmering water that has been rippled
by the slightest touch of wind.

My Own Altar

I worship at the altar of the past,
where pictures stand as icons
and memories are the tabernacle
of prayer. Statues of Mary
protect the area, and small
silver medals of a myriad of saints
stand guard near a gilded triptych.

It is a monument to youth, my own
in particular, celebrating the years
of agility and clear thinking. Pictures
attest to this, darker hair, a thinner body,
devoted to activities that would now call
for a balm at the end of the day,
and no hope to reincarnate
my former physical self.

Dust accumulates over this small space,
I wipe away time as I move each piece.
There are feelings of nostalgia
regret and hindsight mostly, that perfect
vision into what went before, now clearly
understood, measured and weighed
for what it was, or wasn't. But really
it is just the past, gone forever
no matter how cherished, unrepeatable,
and still no forgiveness in sight.

Box of Prayers and Wishes

She showed us the pictures
from the Shinto shrine
near Tokyo, told us how
she had stumbled onto the tail-end
of a wedding party that spring day,
leaving their slim wooden sticks
in the box for prayers and wishes.
The deliberate appointment
of the Japanese calligraphy
had struck her for its beauty,
made her wonder what
this bride and groom had
so carefully printed
on this, their day of days. What
were their secret prayers?
A happy life? Perfect marriage?
Beautiful children? She wished
them all of it, and more,
as she stepped out among
the fallen blossoms
that were strewn across her path.

Faithless

Go ahead, resurrect me, raise me up
from this place that I have gotten to.
Push back the stone and let in the light,
wash my wounds and carry me home.
Or put me on the streets of Rome,
let me stand as a martyr in her catacombs,
among the sacred dead.

I will live for whatever you believe in,
for I cannot stand on my own heart,
which is ever changing, moving away
from its center.

Resurrect me. Take me
to the streets of Jerusalem, seek
the truth there. Find the empty
sepulcher and let me fill it
with the notion of faith that never
finds its way to me. Raise me up
so I can believe what they
already know.

Simply Living

Summer days have shifted into long
dry bouts of unfailing sunlight,
to the point that most of us are begging
for days of rain, itching for the sky
to blacken and bang around some thunder,
light itself up in electrical splendor.
I have slipped through these months
unscathed, opening and closing my days
with no fanfare, rather taking subtlety
to its extreme. Quiet mornings, long
work days, evenings that do not generate
much wattage. I sense I am the better for it,
see that this simple way of passing days
has merit, could even teach me something
about how life goes at times, one moment
to the next, unannounced.

To a Son, Gone to Start His Life

Your bowling shoes sit discarded
in the corner by the front door,
testament to your departure
from this place, gone
to the mountains out east,
looking for your own yin
and yang.

The piano sits silent, another thing
discarded. Left behind in our hands
it is unused, but not disregarded. We hold
instead the memory of melodies
coaxed from its keys by your hands,
now devoted to the simpler tasks of living.

Children ebb and flow through a house,
witness to the uncertainty of life.
They come with no expectations
of what they might receive, or come to know.
But this has been rich and full, this place
you are leaving, and all of us the better for it.

Your Old Garden

I traced the parameter of your old garden today
with the lawnmower, laying the yard to rest

for the winter. Though it's been four years
since you last planted, we had volunteer

cherry tomatoes for two years in a row.
I thought of you each time I brought in a handful.

You had such hopes for that garden,
your first and last. I imagined

you'd find a way to have another
when you finally moved to India.

You planted your feet there, firmly, instead.
And I see that you've grown, too, thrived

as a garden does when it's planted just right,
partial to the sun, with no expectations.

Copper Cup

Your copper cup rests
on the window sill
in the kitchen,
left behind
on your last trip here.

Since then
you have taken a new name,
walked through mountains
in Tibet
and not once called home.

Still, I take the cup
down from the sill,
grasp it tightly
as I pour the wine, say
a short plea that you
will somehow hear this:

Son, in the name of the father
who longs to see you, the mother
who begrudgingly let go of you,
we, who sent you off into the world,
our blessing whispered in your ear,
we say drink deeply from your own cup now,
taste the slight bitterness
left in the last sip, and remember us.

The Dust of Ancient Roads

You were moving towards us, even
as I had the dream, you clad in silver
and Nehru collars, a contemplative heart
coming to tell us just how
you would spend your incredible life.

I wept in my dream, a mother uncertain
of what she has done or will do. It's as if
you grew up away from me, taken in
by the mystical unknown that whispered
in your ear the possibilities if only you'd
let go.

So you did. You let go and fell off the side
of my world and landed
in the jungle, where rogue elephants stomp
at the gates. You bathe there now in lingual waters
tempered by chanting from the temple nearby.
You listen to the rhythmic pulse
and answer its call, sandaled feet moving
through the dust of ancient roads.

Endless Night

In the darkness you come to me,
through the cold and snow,
through endless night, you are there.
It is not always a dream. Sometimes
your presence takes up the room,
moves in and nudges other thoughts aside.

And then I do dream of you, perfectly.
The hotel in Paris, you speaking quietly
to the concierge, tall and straight
and old beyond your years. I see you
through the window of the taxi,
and then inexplicably you disappear,
but there you are again, asleep on a bench,
in a garden. Or are you meditating? The dream
doesn't care about such details,
it records the images and I
play them back over and over.

If I could conjure you up at will,
I would. Instead you follow
your own haunting whims. You're
like a ghost, but still alive somewhere
on this planet, rising each morning
to the shift of earth on its axis,
quieting your breathing until it matches
the pace of your heart.

Ashes of Desire

Flower buds will always remind me
of your puja, the little altar
you adorned each day with delicate
flowers and luscious fruits, the offerings
of a young man, to no gods
in particular, just worshiping
the notion of life as good.
You lit the candles
with such reverence, pulled your body
into the yoga position that best
held you as you chanted your way
to bliss. You smudged your forehead
with vibhuti, the ashes, you said,
of desire, and then simply closed
your beautiful eyes and breathed.

Finding You

The voices of the dead speak to me
quietly, nagging me into wondering
how I will find you among the one
billion who live where you live. How
will I push through this mass of people
and track down one tall, slim, wisp
of a young man? There are no
distinguishing marks on you yet,
just the angle of your walk
as you carry yourself
the way that I will know you.

The voices tell me to come for you,
find you and sit you down
on the side of the road you travel on,
halt you in your certain unfailing steps,
tell you that mistakes have been made
but can be undone, the life you want
can be had closer to home, you can wander
among us, go out into the wilds here,
alone and unchallenged. The dead
are wanting to know that you are near.

To Kailash: On the Back Roads of Tibet

The peak of Mount Kailash rises up in your pictures,
snow-covered even in summer, monolith-like,
iconic. They say the Hindu pilgrims
sometimes circle it, from one
prostration to the next, face down, humbled
at its circumference, and that it can take
them weeks to complete their journey.
It is considered an honor to have done it,
to lay yourself down over and over as you hide
your face in the shadow of such a mountain.

You go there now, to this *axis mundi,*
taking the back roads through Tibet, crossing
its wide open plateaus in rugged SUV's,
heading toward Lhasa, that Shangri la city
you read about in books. But your photographs
show it is not so different than any other city
in modern Asia, cars on paved roads that wind
past palaces and temples from another
incarnation. You walk among the people
as if you had lived there all of your life.

The myth of this holy place exceeds its mystery
and your journey there is both sacred and willful,
to rise up as the moon takes its place in the sky
beside this mountain, and know where you have been,
and how to find your own way back.

Channeling Her Father: A View From Fountain Square

Today my true compass seeks north
as the lace of mist lifts
from tall buildings
and a sun-burned sky shows up.
Edging the street by the fountain
I have tentatively found my footing –
a good girl, channeling her father,
remnants of his memory
flapping like prayer flags in the back of my brain.

I have come here time after time seeking you –
Poppa, Daddy, Big Bob, Father, the shaman
who would lead me
from the old tobacco shop on Virginia Avenue
to that haywire house up north and tell me
how we got there, draw me a map
that follows the convoluted route of misgivings
you stumbled down
when you left your childhood home near the square.

I'm older now, I know.
I'm supposed to leave you to rest,
a ghost aloft in this place, benevolent and succored.
But I need to invoke you here, on this day,
call you up and count you
as my father – name you as the one
responsible for those tricky little defects
in my character DNA, the one who sent me out
to panhandle the universe
for some fatherly advice, some astute guidance

through the slippery slopes
of this middle-aged life.

I quiet myself here
as I peer in the window of the old tobacco shop.
It's an insurance place now, no trace of you
or your life left here, and no hint
of the pathos that reigned later.
There is no secret map left for me to find,
only the spirit of you to fathom.

Whatever They Could Grasp

These hands, I've had them
all my life, yet they appear
now as someone else's,
not mine, but someone older,
the skin thinner, mottled,
a fine white dryness visible,
a tracing of veins, reddened
knuckles that look worked over,
as if by some task done
for many years.

My hands have turned over
a baby or two, lifted
a dying mother, and pounded
a typewriter. I have calluses
from pencils, uneven nails,
and scraggly cuticles. No contest
would be won with these, and yet
my mother told me once
they were beautiful.

I remember her hands when she
was older, the dimpled knuckles,
the scar that ran along her finger,
a nursing school accident, she'd said.
Her hands were smooth and soft
and unwavering.

But there is nothing special here,
just two old hands that have pulled
me, and touched you, and held onto
whatever they could grasp.

Tender and Close

The world feels tender
and close right now.
The baby, resting
in my daughter's arms,
makes it so.

We sit on the bench outside
the coffee shop watching
the blue sky dim
as evening comes on.
In such simplicity
we are moved forward,
second to second,
generation
to generation.

I have
unbound my love
again, as deeply as
the first time.

Where is Your Placenta Buried?

If we were good keepers
of the Seri language we'd know
this is a most important question.
It will tell us where we are from,
and how far we have come.

I happen to know where yours
is buried, from the mystical story
of your birth, the picture
of your father and the doctor drinking
at the kitchen table while you labored
to be born in the room just above them
ingrained in my memory as if
it were my own, and now it is myth
in our family, the story we told our kids
when they were younger so they
would have a real sense of you.

Your dad and the old doctor
drank themselves silly while
the Christian Science midwife
brought you into this world,
the last of five and the only one
your mother birthed
as her faith directed.

They buried your placenta under
the sugar maple in the side yard, a tree
I can pass by on a good walk any day.
Comforting to know that we know
exactly where you are from.

Biking to Versailles

Biking to Versailles, even the rain
couldn't stop us, relentless as it was.
The market in town, still open
despite the torrent, offered up the same
dizzying display of jeweled pastries
and enviable cheese choices as if
it were a perfect day in August
with clear skies and pristine sun. As it was,
we stuffed our backpacks with fromage
encrusted with golden raisins, and wrapped
delicate pear tarts in wax paper, destined
for the driest depths of those packs, hopeful
as we were for a luncheon refuge. We found it
under the bent awnings of a closed café,
and there shared a repast of exquisite tastes.
Sodden riders passed brie and baguettes,
olives and figs found their way among us, the rich smoky
charcuteries were gently unfolded from their wrappings.

And the palace rose behind us, embraced
by acres of gardens and ponds, defying the rain
and standing resplendent despite it
while the peasants at its gates ate like kings.

The Light Within

Here is the spirit's rest:
I can breathe in through this thought
all that went before this moment,
the errands, fixing the meal together,
your thoughts about your brother,
still so far from home, yet here among us now,
and your belief that makes it so. I can rest too,
knowing that darkness will bring comfort,
a velvet wrap against the cool breeze
that comes up as the light wanes.

We hold on a moment more, to the hushed
conversation that passes between us all,
before we rise to go inside,
the light within that beckons us
bright and warm.

And this is day's end here, you and your boy
quietly counting toes, fresh from the grass,
his laughter melodic as we start
to put our things away.

January Light

Morning light lingers over
the rooftops of the houses

on my street. Winter break
almost over, I get up early

for practice. I see the world
just a bit differently

at this time of day.
Houses stand dark, as contrast

to the yellow blue light
around them. I go to retrieve

the newspaper and find that all
is quiet in my yard.

the world is not yet up,
only me in my house shoes

and pajamas, roaming the yard,
seeking news of the world.

Equinox

All winter I've watched the light,
pondered it, commiserated about it,
ached for it, and mourned its passing.

Today I quiet myself to listen, hoping
to capture the slightest creak or groan
of movement as earth shifts herself
into alignment, heaves her axis up
to just the right degree of angle, so
that we can split night in half,

break the line of darkness with at least
the subtleness of shadows, break it open
to bring on the day.

ACKNOWLEDGEMENTS

The authors thank the publications in which some of these poems, or versions thereof, first appeared.

Part I — THE UMBRELLA SHORE, by Jayne Marek

A Lost Country	*The Occasional Reader* (Roslyn, Washington)
The Buckskin	*Community Breeze* (Silver Lake, Oregon)
Fitting	*Prism* (Tacoma, Washington)
Invitation	*Saxifrage*
Range in the Stars	*Driftwood Bay*
Trapping Season	*Isthmus*
The Umbrella Shore	*The Bend*

Part II — WHAT SHE TAUGHT ME, by Lylanne Musselman

Lost Art	*Birds Eye reView*
Ode to Aging Baby Boomers	*Ichabod's Sketchbook IV*
On Seagulls	*Deep Waters* (Outrider Press Anthology 2012)
Take Back Time	*Birds Eye reView*
Wasting Away in Compositionville	*Literary Brushstrokes*

Part III — MEMORIES OF AN UNARCHIVED PAST, by Mary Sexson

Ashes of Desire	*Cincinnati Writers Project Anthology* (2012)
Box of Prayers and Wishes	*Trip of a Lifetime* (2012)
Channeling Her Father	Masterpiece in a Day second prize winner (Indianapolis, 2010)
The Dust of Ancient Roads	*Tipton Poetry Journal*
Equinox	*Cincinnati Writers Project Anthology* (2012)
Your Old Garden	*Ichabod's Sketchbook IV*

BIOGRAPHICAL NOTES

 The pond out back provides **Jayne Marek** with daily glimpses of nature's beauty and drama. Her poems have appeared in publications such as *Lantern Journal, Siren, Spillway, Driftwood Bay, Tipton Poetry Journal, Isthmus, The Occasional Reader, Wisconsin Academy Review,* and *Windless Orchard* and in anthologies: *And Know This Place: Poetry of Indiana* and the 2012 Cincinnati Writers Project collection. Her chapbook *Imposition of Form on the Natural World* was brought out by Finishing Line Press early in 2013. Marek also publishes fiction, photographs, and feature articles. Her one-act play "Katherine and Virginia," which characterizes the friendship between authors Katherine Mansfield and Virginia Woolf, has been performed in New York City and Indiana, and she was a featured playwright at the Oaklandon Civic Theatre's spring short play festival in 2006. She teaches courses in literature, writing, and film at Franklin College.

Lylanne Musselman is an award-winning poet, artist, and playwright. She's worked as a waitress, a glass bander, a paper maker, a float builder and parade float driver, a typesetter, an art instructor, and a caricaturist before finding her passion – writing poems. To support her poetry habit, Musselman teaches writing of all stripes at Terra State and Ivy Tech Community Colleges. Her poems have appeared or are forthcoming in *Tipton Poetry Journal, Pank, Umbrella, The Prose-Poem Project,* and *The Rusty Nail* among others, and many anthologies. She is the author of three chapbooks: *Prickly Beer and Purple Panties* (Bacon Tree Press, 2007), *A Charm Bracelet For Cruising* (Winged City Press, 2009) and *Winged Graffiti* (Finishing Line Press, 2011). Her one-act play "Surfacing" has been performed at Ball State University and her monologue "Of Mother and Men" appears in *Mother/Daughter Monologues Volume 2: Thirtysomethings.* A native Hoosier, Musselman now resides in Toledo, Ohio, with her three cats, Graham, Tink, and Fiyero.

 **Mary Sexson** is the author of the book *103 in the Light, Selected Poems 1996-2000*, (Restoration Press, 2004), nominated by the Indiana Center for the Book for a Best Books of Indiana award in poetry in 2005. Her work has been included in the IndyGo Shared Voices/Shared Spaces poetry project, Arts Kaleidoscope, Masterpiece in a Day, the Poetry in Paint project at the Garfield Park Arts Center, and the Poetry in Free Motion Project (September, 2012). Her poems have appeared in *Flying Island, Borders Insight Magazine, Grasslands Review*, the *Tipton Poetry Journal, The Globetrotter's Companion* (UK), and a special Kurt Vonnegut edition of *The Tipton Poetry Journal*: *One City, One Prompt*. Her latest work can be seen in the Cincinnati Writers Project 2012 Anthology and the *Trip of a Lifetime* Anthology (Sleeping Cat Books), December 2012.